THE JOY OF EX

don't get mad – get over it

Vicky Edwards

summersdale

THE JOY OF EX

Copyright © Summersdale Publishers Ltd 2005
Text by Vicky Edwards
Illustrations by Alex Hallatt

Summersdale Publishers Ltd
46 West Street
Chichester
West Sussex
PO19 1RP
UK

www.summersdale.com

Printed and bound by Proost, Belgium

ISBN 1 84024 409 7

About the author

Vicky Edwards is a writer and broadcaster. She is also the not-so-proud owner of a back-catalogue of disastrous love affairs with totally unsuitable men. However, since she started taking her own advice, everything in her romantic garden has come up roses and she is now married to the world's most perfect man and has just had her first baby. But she is not in the least bit smug.

For The Maggot, with grateful thanks for making me sufficiently miserable that I was able to decide that enough was most definitely enough.

Contents

Introduction

Even if it wasn't the love affair of the century, nobody enjoys being given the sack in a relationship. At best, the ego suffers slight bruising and, at the other end of the emotional spectrum, the pain is akin to having major surgery performed by Darth Vader without the benefit of anaesthetic.

The days immediately following a break-up can be dark and difficult, and it's nigh on impossible to believe that you will not only get through the tunnel of despair, but that you will cheerfully skip down the tunnel of love again. But hold the latter part of that thought. Separation *can* be, ultimately, a positive experience. It can be an opportunity to break bad relationship habits ('Why do I always end up with a heartless bastard/bitch?') and a chance to gain emotional maturity and greater self-awareness. Yes, it requires spadework (at a time when all you probably want to dig is a big hole to climb into), but if you're willing to make the effort then there are some juicy rewards on offer. Not only will you be likely to make better relationship choices in the future, but you can also really learn to enjoy the benefits of your single status too.

This book is aimed, primarily, at women who have yet to shimmy up the aisle. However, the principles of the following pages are relevant to anyone, male or female, married or not, who is struggling with the misery, anger and bewilderment that comes with rejection and heartbreak.

Chapter One

Being dumped

The first 24 hours following the final curtain of a relationship are crucial for the person who is at the sharp end of the break-up. People have been known to make matters much worse for themselves by taking drastic/ silly/illegal/alcohol-fuelled action in the immediate aftermath of being given their cards. The following rules apply in general after being dumped, but *especially* in the first

24 hours when emotions are at their peak and you are spitting blood with rage and/or a sobbing mess.

Do

DO... SORT OUT THE FUNDAMENTAL DOMESTIC ARRANGEMENTS AS SOON AS POSSIBLE

If you have been sharing the same home then the sooner one of you can vacate the premises the better for both of you. If there are children involved then great sensitivity to their emotional state is needed. The impartial support of family on both sides is enormously helpful to children at this time and even if you and your Ex can agree on nothing else, you should be united in all matters concerning your children's happiness and well-being.

DO... GRIEVE

Bawling your eyes out is far healthier than bottling your feelings up and pretending that you're fine (remember that 'FINE' stands for F***ed-up, Insecure, Neurotic and Emotional!). If you think you would feel better for having a shoulder to cry on then ask a close friend to stay for a day or two, or arrange to go to their place. You might not want to talk but there is a lot to be said for even the silent support of someone who cares about you when you are at your lowest ebb and have as many Kleenex on the go as Carrie Bradshaw has shoes in her closet.

DO... EXPRESS YOUR FEELINGS CONSTRUCTIVELY

One of the best ways to do this is to punch hell out of a pile of cushions. It might sound bonkers, and you might feel a bit of an imbecile bashing seven shades out of Ikea's finest, but once you get stuck into it you will find such violent exertions extremely satisfying. Just imagine the cushions represent the unfairness of the situation in which you find yourself. Or maybe your Ex's head/genitals/the third party that came between you.

DO... TAKE CARE OF YOURSELF

THIS MEANS:

1. Eating even when you don't feel like it.
2. Going to bed and trying to sleep even when you would rather stay up all night howling along to 'your song'.
3. Washing yourself and your clothes when you would prefer to soap-dodge on the sofa in a scuzzy old T-shirt.
4. Taking some gentle exercise when it's much easier to be flat on your back in bed feeling the tears running into your ears.

Remember!
Self-care equals self-respect and you are going to need as much of this as you can muster.

DO... ACCEPT ANY PART IN THE DEMISE OF THE RELATIONSHIP FOR WHICH YOU ARE REPONSIBLE

Were you too possessive? Did you have fits of jealousy for no good reason? Were you argumentative simply to provoke a reaction? Be brutally honest with yourself and if any of these negative traits apply to you then resolve to address the root cause of such behaviour and to do things differently in the future. (Unless of course your Ex is completely responsible for the break-up, in which case it's more helpful to accept that they are a complete ratbag and return to the cushion-bashing with an even more colourful vocabulary.)

DO... TAKE IT A DAY AT A TIME

You wouldn't expect to be up and about and running a marathon the day after you'd broken your leg, so why on earth should you be on top form when your heart feels like it's been used as a trampoline by a stampeding herd of over-excited rhinos? Recovery from emotional stress takes as long as broken bones do to mend, so be patient with yourself.

DO... KNOW YOUR SOCIAL LIMITS

It is vital not to shut yourself away from the world, but don't accept invitations that you know you will simply find too much to cope with in the early days. Weddings, for instance, unless you are a complete masochist, are probably best avoided.

Don't

DON'T... MAKE PLEADING/THREATENING/
DRUNKEN PHONE CALLS TO YOUR EX

If you think you are likely to find this difficult then hand over your mobile to a mate, get them to police your outgoing calls from the landline and denude your purse of all coinage accepted by telephone boxes.

DON'T... DESTROY ANY PHOTOS, LETTERS, GIFTS OR ANY OF YOUR EX'S POSSESSIONS IN THE FIRST WEEK OR SO OF BREAKING UP

In subsequent weeks you may find it helpful to get rid of mementoes (see *Heartbreak therapies*) but wanton destruction carried out in the heat of the moment often results in a self-kicking later on. Apart from maybe wanting to review the personal items when you are feeling calmer, trashing your Ex's clothes and gear could land you in serious trouble. It also makes you look like a Bunny Boiler. Settle for packing painful reminders away in the short term. As regards gifts, well, think about it; some of them might be saleable. And while flogging them now and buying sassy undies for someone else's benefit with the proceeds might seem unthinkable, in a month or so you might get a really positive 'moving on' buzz out of such a transaction.

DON'T... GET OFF YOUR FACE

Fact: alcohol and drugs are depressants and you definitely don't need any further help in this direction. Although the idea of oblivion might be attractive, when you sober up things will be just as bad as they were before, plus, physically, you'll feel like death's-head-on-a-mop-stick. Being trollied is never a good plan at break-up time, as it is in this state that you usually decide to ring or visit your Ex. Apart from making a tit of yourself, no Ex has ever taken someone back after having neat vodka or six pints of Stella vomited on their shoes...

DON'T... BAD-MOUTH YOUR EX TO THEIR FAMILY AND FRIENDS

It might bring you a few moments' light relief but it will do you no favours whatsoever in the long term. You will only succeed in embarrassing these people and making them want to sprint in the opposite direction when they see you coming in the future.

DON'T... PLAY GAMES

Keeping your dignity will help you to recover more quickly and turning up at places where you know your Ex will be 'by accident' fools nobody and only makes you look desperate and pathetic. The same goes for contacting your Ex and inventing reasons to meet up. Apart from legitimate queries about joint possessions and domestic arrangements, keep contact to an absolute minimum. This way you won't have the opportunity to do all those self-destructive things. Like asking if they are seeing anybody else. You'll also be better placed to avoid the biggest no-no of all…

DON'T... SLEEP WITH YOUR EX

This means having to live through those initial and most painful feelings of rejection all over again, as it is almost a foregone conclusion that they won't change their mind about the fact that it is O-V-E-R just because you've had a post-split bunk-up.

DON'T... SLEEP WITH ANYONE WHO IS UP FOR A ONE-NIGHT-ONLY BIT OF JIGGY-JIGGY

Launching yourself into a frenzy of casual sex and one-night-stands will be as useful to you as a bar of chocolate in a sauna. You sure as hell won't find your self-esteem under somebody else's pillow and the pain, shame and embarrassment of waking up next to something Jurassic the next morning will be hideous. Being in the wrong place with the wrong person way too soon after a major break-up will do nothing more for your state of mind than make you feel like a bit of a slapper.

Ex Factors

'Love is the great
incentive – not just sex'

Michael **C**aine

Ex Factors

'Expecting life to treat you well because you are a good person is like expecting an angry bull not to charge because you are a vegetarian'

SHARI **R B**ARR

Or in other words: Shit happens to us all

Chapter Two

Tapping into your resources

If breaking up is hard to do then dredging up the motivation to tap into your positive resources can be even harder. The simple reason for this is that feeling miserably post-dumped is a deep quagmire from which to stir yourself. Again, it's back to self-care and you will need to give yourself a dose of tough love, get your arse into gear and do things that will nurture you.

FRIENDS

At a time like this you really need the support of your mates. Don't be afraid to ask for it. Real friends understand that you might not feel up to partying and will be willing to stay in with you. Real friends will listen when you need to talk and won't be judgmental of you. Real friends will turn up on your doorstep with their own body weight in pick 'n' mix on the night that *Sleepless in Seattle* is scheduled in the TV listings and you are going to be home alone.

FOOD

A lot of people, women especially, tend to go one way or the other with food following a break-up. Some find that misery kills their appetite stone dead and slinky hips become the only plus point of being dumped. For others it is a trigger for the Cream Cake Roadshow to commence, and then it's downhill all the way to feeling rejected AND fat. Neither of these attitudes are healthy and you really do need to eat as well as you can. As with exercise, a healthy diet will promote a better overall sense of well-being. Although a few lapses involving your favourite comfort foods won't do any harm.

PHYSICAL EXERCISE

This can be a great way to lift your spirits. As well as providing a physical release for your anger, it gets the blood pumping and the endorphins going. The main effect is a much-improved state of mind and body, which is a distinctly better place from which to move forwards. If the gym or running is your idea of purgatory then a few lengths of the swimming pool, a good flinging of yourself around the dance floor, a spot of kick boxing or half an hour of brisk walking will do the trick just as well. Think of it as 'Walking Back to Happiness'!

Ex Factors

'The best way to cheer
yourself up is to try to
cheer somebody else up'

MARK **T**WAIN

BLEACH

A good cleaning session, furniture rearrangement and clearing out of cupboards can produce an incredibly cathartic effect.

Case Study

'At the end of a relationship I turn to manic house cleaning. I find zooming through my house like a whirling dervish, relentlessly destroying every innocent dust particle, piece of paper or item of clothing that no longer serves a useful purpose in my life, enormously satisfying. I also end up with a lovely clean place in which to mend my broken heart. But as I have just got married, I really hope to have a pretty grubby house for many years to come!'

Kimberly, a businesswoman, aged 29

TALENTS AND SKILLS

Throw yourself into hobbies. Creativity is a wonderful well in which to deposit negative emotions so whether it's pottery, poetry, making clothes, rebuilding cars, arm wrestling or flower arranging, the distraction of concentrating on something other than your Ex, especially when coupled with the actual act of creating something, can be another great mood-lifter.

Ex Factors

Positive Affirmations

Pick one of the following, or make one of
your own up, and say it twenty times to
yourself every morning whilst in the bath
or shower.

I am loved and loveable

I am beautiful

I am healthy and happy

I am in control of my life

I think before taking action

I am free

I welcome the opportunity to grow

Bad things don't happen to me any more

My Ex will get a nasty dose of something
from the next person they sleep with…
Oops! Only joking

Ex Factors

Don't have any truck with the 'let's stay friends' cliché. It might sound tough but only in a tiny handful of instances does this optimistic phrase translate into reality. The harsh fact is that it is simply too painful to try and be friends with someone you still love and you are much better advised to cut the cord swiftly. Maybe, in time, a friendship can be developed – but that is something to think about much later on.

Chapter Three

They think it's all over:
Telling people

The first thing to be aware of is that some people will, inevitably, want to know 'the full story' of the break-up. In essence this boils down to 'Whose fault was it?' Decide what you want to do. Do you want to tell them the full story? Or would you prefer to just let it go at something like 'It was a mutual decision', or, 'He left me but I don't really want to go into the details'? Whatever you decide don't be bullied into spilling your emotional beans unless you want to. Not everyone is discreet and unless you want to become the subject of idle gossip, choose your confidants carefully.

If you can't face repeating yourself every time you talk to or meet a friend, colleague or family member, then the modern world offers a simple solution: send a short text or e-mail to everyone in your address books. It doesn't need to be a diatribe that includes all the gory details, and you should make a point of clarifying what kind of response you would like.

Send a short text or e-mail to everyone in your address books.

A couple of examples:

THE MATURE AND DIGNIFIED APPROACH

Dear all,

Just a quick note to let you know that, sadly, Tom and I have parted company. It will take a bit of getting used to, but I'm OK. I'm trying to stay busy and cheerful so if anyone fancies lunch, dinner or a night out then it would be lovely to hear from you.

THE NOT-SO-MATURE-AND-DIGNIFIED APPROACH

Dear all,

Just a quick note to let you know that if you see that bastard Tom, feel free to kick him in the nuts. The two-timing git has been seeing that Julie from his office for the last two months. I'm trying to stay busy and cheerful by studying a voodoo correspondence course, so if anyone fancies joining me for a bit of well-aimed pin-sticking then it would be lovely to hear from you.

Alternatively, if you're REALLY angry (and have some spare cash) you could consider taking out a newspaper ad or signing up for bus/tube advertising.

All joking aside, do ensure that you tell those who will support you best as soon as you can and don't, whatever you do, lie or embellish the reasons for a break-up. Lies like this have a nasty habit of coming back and biting you on the bum.

Case Study

*'In the initial stages of heartbreak I treat myself
as I would an invalid – home-made soup, duvet
on the sofa and loads of self-administered TLC.
Once the shock has subsided my next step is
to get into the garden and dig for Britain. The
combination of the physical effort involved, the
smell of the earth and the toiling for something
that will eventually grow and flourish leaves me
feeling tired but peaceful.'*

Jessica, an artist, aged 28

Chapter Four

The spoils of war:
Who gets what?

If living apart then arrange to exchange possessions as soon as you can. If this presents an awkward situation, enlist the assistance of a mutual friend.

If living together, keep it absolutely fair and square. Any joint purchases should be split fifty-fifty. If this creates tension and confrontation then see if a mutual friend is willing to act as a mediator.

EXPENSIVE PRESENTS

The general rule of thumb is that a gift is a gift – unless you gave each other family heirlooms on the basis that you were going to be together forever, in which case such items should be given back.

Case Study

'When Roy and I split up – his choice, not mine – I asked for a silver cigar box that had belonged to my late grandfather back, and which I had given to Roy when we got engaged. I'd given it in anticipation of our being together forever and for him, in turn, to pass down to our children. He was absolutely fine about it and even better, when I offered him his ring back, which seemed the right thing to do, he refused. I later sold it and bought a fabulous designer outfit which I wore to a wedding... where I promptly pulled my lovely husband!'

Lesley, a nurse, aged 32

Ex Factors

'Regret is an appalling
waste of energy – you
can't build on it; it's only
good for wallowing in'

Katherine **M**ansfield

Chapter Five

Heartbreak therapies

CREDIT CARD CALMING

Whilst running up a host of debts is not so smart, a one-off spend on good, esteem-boosting treats is perfectly acceptable and can be a ray of light in your pit of despondency. Now is definitely the time to indulge yourself so even if it means breaking into savings or going temporarily into the red, get out there and pamper yourself with whatever sort of loveliness floats your boat.

For instance, what could you splurge on which will help you feel any better about your post-break-up self?

- A make-over
- A spa day
- A fabulous dress
- A CD frenzy
- A new car
- A holiday
- A course in something that you have always wanted to do
- A personal development seminar
- A beautiful piece of jewellery

- Tickets to see a concert or show for you and a mate
- Designer underwear
- Wickedly expensive perfume
- A wonderful painting or sketch
- A few laps around a race track in a Ferrari
- Hot air balloon trip
- Shoes to die for

Case Study

'When Gary left me I was so distraught that I barely went out for the first month. But then a dear friend persuaded me to spend a day being massaged and pampered at a health farm and it really made me feel like a new woman. After that I booked myself in for some sort of treat every weekend for the following two months. Having something to look forward to at the end of each week that was an indulgence and a kindness to myself really did make a big difference to my emotional recovery and was worth every last penny.'

Emma, a radio presenter, aged 25

Case Study

'When I split with my last Ex, a very domineering guy who I'd allowed to erode my self-confidence simply by being daft enough to stay with him, I decided to treat myself. I booked onto a course of singing lessons with a professional who specialised in teaching 'shy' vocalists and it was like someone had turned the lights on inside of me. I'll never be a Pop Idol but I LOVE singing! It's boosted my self-confidence and given me a whole new social circle, as now I sing regularly with a choir and have met loads of new, fun and interesting people as a result.'

Kelly, a florist, aged 36

VIRTUAL REVENGE

There have been plenty of well-documented revenge tales over the years. Clothes being cut in half, expensive cars being plastered in pink paint and, of course, the constant stream of celebrity splits, which usually entail people stinging former partners for millions and squealing to the tabloid press. But as mentioned earlier, actually damaging your Ex's property or causing them physical harm is more likely to land you in court than have any long-term positive effect on your life. HOWEVER! There's a world apart between thinking and acting out your fantasies. *Virtual* revenge is an excellent way to expel anger.

It's also a good way of spending time with friends and having a laugh – always welcome when you have a permanent headache from crying and the corners of your mouth have forgotten how to turn up.

Some stories of revenge to
cheer you up
(DO NOT TRY THESE AT HOME)

KNICKERS WITH A TWIST

It's said that technology is a wonderful thing – and John couldn't agree more. When he thought that his wife, Lisa, was getting her jollies elsewhere, he took it upon himself to advertise 'a handful of my cheating wife's knickers' for sale on a popular consumer website. Lisa, suffice to say, was suitably mortified.

A HANDFUL OF MY CHEATING WIFE'S KNICKERS
£20.00

BIDDING ENDS TODAY

THE SEEDS OF REVENGE

A woman was dumped by a man that she had been very much in love with. To add insult to injury, he asked her, a month after dumping her, if she would pop into his new flat to collect his post and water his plants while he was away on holiday. He had just had a very expensive new carpet fitted in his living room and the arrogant toad instructed the poor woman to ensure that she took her shoes off before entering this room. Once she meekly agreed to do what he asked, he gave her the keys and waltzed off to the Canaries with his new girlfriend. Our poor rejected damsel then smiled quietly to herself, and every night for a fortnight let herself into his flat and busied herself. Upon his return in the small hours of the morning her Ex discovered a lawn of mustard and cress growing in his beautiful new carpet. In an inspired act of revenge his 'doormat' of an ex-girlfriend had sown the entire carpet with seeds before his flight had even left Gatwick, and had diligently spent every night until his return watering her 'garden'. Evidently his shrieks could be heard five streets away.

After an acrimonious split in which Sharon left her fiancé, Michael, for Michael's best friend, the injured party decided to exact his revenge. He discovered the couple's new address through mutual friends and then settled down to bide his time. After three months he discovered that they were going to a wedding in Jamaica and would be gone for a fortnight. Michael knew that there was one thing that terrified the living daylights out of Sharon: mice. Having watched them drive off to the airport from his hiding place of the bus shelter on the other side of the street, he approached the front door and posted through the letterbox a male mouse and a female mouse. Every night for two weeks, under the cover of darkness, he returned to pop food through the letterbox. He heard from one of his colleagues who was a good friend of his Ex's that she had fainted with shock when she arrived home to an infestation of mice, which had also managed to chew through the telephone, computer and hi-fi cables and make a nest in the duvet.

Another good way of having virtual revenge
is to indulge in:

SAFE SPLEEN VENTING

YOU WILL NEED:
1. Some friends with vivid imaginations
2. A couple of bottles of wine
3. Cheesy nibbles of your choice

INSTRUCTIONS:

Pick a night when you would otherwise be doing nothing more constructive than crying into your M&S dinner-for-one and invite some mates round. The challenge is to take it in turns to come up with the most outrageous insults and tortures for your Ex, highlighting anything that they were especially sensitive about – big nose, small willy, spotty botty etc.

A cleansing heartbreak therapy that has helped many a chuckee is a good burn-up. You need to ensure that you are ready to part with the souvenirs of your romance, but if you have satisfied yourself that this is the case then it's time for:

YOU WILL NEED:

1. Kindling
2. Fire-lighters
3. Matches
4. A secluded back garden or a fireplace (conducive weather conditions if the former)
5. Love letters or mementoes of your Ex that you are sure you want rid of
6. Some friends
7. A couple of bottles of wine
8. Marshmallows and skewers

INSTRUCTIONS:

Build your fire and then add the letters, gifts, keepsakes and photographs. Light the fire carefully. When it has taken hold and your past with your Ex is flaming nicely, raise a glass and get everyone to drink to your future health, happiness and flourishing love life. Pass round the skewers and marshmallows and get toasting (imagining that the confectionery represents a part of your Ex's anatomy).

HARD LINES

The pen is mightier than the sword and another helpful way of alleviating your fury or despair is to write a letter to your Ex, telling them exactly, in no uncertain terms, *why* you are angry with them. Hold nothing back. If you're seething then use whatever language you want, name-call to your heart's content, let home truths flow freely, hit well and truly below the belt (if they were a crap shag go right ahead and put it down in black and white) and insult their friends and family. If you are just distraught and all you want to do is write how much you love them, want them back and can't live without them, then get it all down on the page, along with copious tear stains.

The next part of this particular therapy is very, *very* important: **when you have written your letter, tear it up into extremely small pieces and put it in the bin underneath soggy tea bags and all those snotty tissues you have sobbed into. Under no circumstances is this epistle to be sent.** It is simply the act of writing it down, in this first instance, that provides an escape valve for your anger or misery. Later on, if you need to, you can send a much tempered and more reasonable version. However, you will almost certainly

live to regret sending your first draft so burn
any stamps and envelopes that you might have
in your possession before you pick up your
biro!

Ex Factors

Yesterday's the past,
tomorrow's the future,
but today is a gift. That's
why it's called the present.

In other words: No matter how bad you
feel, make the most of the here and now.

Chapter Six

Starting again

> *Embrace change: shout 'hurrah', wave your knickers in the air and rev up for the new and improved life that is yours for the taking.*

Think of this time as an opportunity to pause and consider a personal update. Think about all the aspects of your life – appearance, attitude, work, friends, hobbies, family, commitments, dreams and ambitions. Now, think about the things within that list that you would like to change. What's stopping you? The short answer in most cases is nothing, so jump to it! If you have always fancied having red hair, being more assertive, becoming a mime artist, ditching some acquaintances with whom you no longer have anything in common, taking up naked parachuting, seeing more of your grandparents, rearranging your finances and running a tea shop, make it happen. Or, to be more practical, take a good long look at the things that would really help you to be happier and fulfilled and set about trying to achieve them.

Part of starting again and the whole personal house-cleaning gig entails addressing previous relationship stumbling blocks. Are you a relationship junkie? Do you only feel 'whole' if you are one half of a pair or if you are 'fixing' someone? Do you have a habit of attracting abusive/using/cheating/insecure partners? Are you prone to being jealous/demanding/flirtatious/moody/argumentative when you are in a relationship? Time to dredge back, see where these problems have their roots, and take some positive action. If it's something that has caused you repeated pain and let-down in the past, maybe it's time to consider…

COUNSELLING

Counselling can be incredibly helpful. Forget the stigma that used to surround visiting 'Trick Cyclists'; in this day and age anybody who is anybody does a stint with a counsellor at some point. However, be warned: any Tom, Dick, Harry or Betty can stick their name in the phone book and call themselves a counsellor, so be sure to check them out first. The best way is to either get a recommendation from your GP or from someone you know and trust and who has been through counselling themselves. There's any amount of different kinds of counselling available today so take the time to consider your needs and to find someone who is going to be right for you.

OTHER PERSONAL DEVELOPMENT AREAS

Like counselling, there are heaps of options in this arena: insight seminars, releasing-the-goddess-within workshops, how-to-get-angry workshops, hypnosis, co-dependency conventions, convent retreats, finding-yourself holidays; you name it, it's out there. Again, do research anything that interests you before signing up and make sure that you are not going to get ripped off or are about to trust someone phony. Apparently the ultimate cleansing experience is colonic irrigation. If you're feeling brave then your nearest Bum Laundry can be located via the telephone directory, but personally I would venture that opting for this particular treatment after a painful break-up just adds insult to injury.

Ex Factors

By all means look back at the past – but only for long enough to learn from it. Don't make the mistake of staring into the past. Staring is not only rude but it distracts you from the happiness of the present and, as a result, opportunities pass by right under your nose.

Ex Factors

A mantra for the recently dumped:

I am worth better, I will have better, soon I will feel better.

(And when I am feeling better I will have his testicles for earrings.)

Case Study

'I was once on holiday in a fabulous place with a man who subsequently dumped me when we got back, but obviously made his mind up during the holiday. I didn't know what was coming, but knew that I was unhappy, and I felt very alone as he spent very little time with me and just made polite conversation when we were together. I was walking along the beach, on my own feeling pretty desolate, when a pelican swooped down into the water and caught a fish right in front of me. It was amazing to see and really lifted my spirits. From then on I have lived my life for the "pelican moments".'

Jacqueline, a mosaics designer, aged 30

Chapter Seven

Reasons to be a joyous ex

• Time to focus on what you want – or don't want – from life and love

• Spending time with old friends and making new ones

• You don't have to tell anyone where you are going or when you'll be back – you're free!

• Flirting

• Nobody else's hair stuck to the soap

• Being able to make starfish shapes in your own bed without someone snoring, farting or nicking the duvet

• No longer having to witness the picking, rummaging and rearranging that goes on at various parts of men's bodies

• Regaining custody and control of the TV remote

• Getting to eat both chops

- Not having to shave one's legs

- No in-laws or partner's friends to worry about, buy presents for or to pretend to like

- The knowledge that ultimately someone else always comes along anyway, whether it takes a few months or a year – or three!

- The toilet seat isn't left up and there's no dribble (urghh)

• You don't have to buy presents for him any more so you'll have more disposable income for clothes and chocolate, hurrah!

• You don't have to go to the pain and expense of having your bits waxed

• You don't feel guilty about fantasising about other men

• When you get home from work, the house will be exactly as you left it and you won't have to redo the washing up, tidy up the newspapers, pick up the clothes and make the bed (again!)

• And most important of all, being single will teach you that happiness begins with you, not with another person.

www.summersdale.com